ONE
DECISION
CAN

DAVE JESIOLOWSKI

Book designed and edited by Sheenah Freitas
papercranebooks.com

ISBN: 978-1515275497 (Paperback)
ISBN: 978-0-578-42021-9 (Hardback)

Printed in the United States of America

For information about special discounts for bulk purchases, please contact special sales at 769-300-6199

To my sons, Jake and Reed. I hope the lessons in this book and the way I have lived my life will inspire you to live life with courage when you're afraid, honesty when you want to lie to avoid hurting someone, patience when you want things to happen faster than you can control, and passion because this is what fuels your dreams. On your journey you will need these, but the most important thing to remember is to love. Love what you do, love yourself, love others when they don't deserve it, and love life. Be grateful. For one day your time on Earth will expire and you will have wanted to enjoy as many moments of your life as possible. Make memories. Make experiences. Most importantly, make a difference. At the end of your life, the only things you will have are the memories and experiences you made. The only things that will live on past your life are the memories and experiences you created for others. May those memories and experiences have made a difference. Be known as a significant person in someone's life. Life is made up of time and emotions. Spend your time being grateful. Enjoy every moment you can. When storms come, and they will, know that they are meant to teach you a lesson that can be shared with others to alleviate suffering.

To my mom who taught me to always believe in myself.

To my dad who taught me that with patience and hard work, you can overcome any adversity.

To my grandmother who taught me how to live life by the way she lived her life

To you the reader of this book. Thank you for investing in this book and yourself so that you can grow personally and professionally. I have invested over 3 decades of my life acquiring the wisdom and knowledge contained within the pages of this book and I promise you, if you will consistently apply what you learn in this book it will change your life ...

Table of Contents

PART 2: SUSTAINABILITY AND CONSISTENCY

Prologue

After playing professional hockey for six seasons, it was time for me to move into the next season of my life. Disappointed that that chapter of my life was closing and uncertain of what life had in store for me next, I asked myself "What am I going to do with the rest of my life?"

I believe we all ask ourselves that same question as we drift from one season of life to the next, but do we ever really stop and think about the answer? **What are you going to do with the rest of your life?** What's your answer? Have you lost sight of the future because of the busyness of life?

Do you want to live your life experiencing **stress, anxiety, guilt, fear, frustration, failure, worry, embarrassment, jealousy, anger, resentment, or regret?**

—OR—

Would you like to be the top person in your profession and be able to truly impact peoples' lives? Would you like to be wealthy and healthy? Would you like to have a great relationship with your spouse or significant other? Do you want to be a great parent and a great leader? What if you could be the best coach, the best athlete, or the best sales person? What if you could experience more joy, freedom, success, happiness, wins, excitement, trust, clarity, confidence, passion, love, hope, faith, and alignment in your life? What if you could have more freedom or a better quality of life?

If that's what people want, then why aren't they doing it?

Why aren't *you* doing it?

The beginning of transformation starts with deciding to change because you're not satisfied with the results you are currently experiencing.

You must have strong enough reasons to act towards your ideal outcome.

What has prevented you in the past from living the life you know you are capable of?

What's preventing you now from living the life you know you are capable of?

Is it time for you to live a life of success and significance?

What's that worth to you?

It's not always easy, but it is always worth it.

What do you really want out of life?

"All we have to decide is what to do with the time that is given to us."

—J.R.R. TOLKIEN,
THE FELLOWSHIP OF THE RING

PART 1: TRANSFORMING YOUR LIFE

CHAPTER 1

Becoming Uncomfortable: Going from Stress to Success

"IN THE MIDST OF CHAOS THERE IS ALSO OPPORTUNITY."

—SUN TZU

MY STORY OF STRUGGLE

When I realized my days of playing professional hockey were over, I felt uncertain about who I was going to be. My whole life, I was always known as a hockey player. So as I entered the next season of my life with uncertainty, confusion, and a new baby on the way, I was thinking, *What's next?*

Little did I know that **the next year would have such a profound impact on the direction of my life.**

When I moved to Jackson, Mississippi from New York after retiring from playing hockey, I worked four different jobs. I opened the YMCA at 4:45 in the morning. I'd leave there at 7:15 and build houses until 3:30 in the afternoon—the hottest part of the day. Being in the sweltering Mississippi heat and humidity was not easy for a guy originally from Edmonton, Alberta, Canada, where the temperatures rarely exceeded 75° Fahrenheit in the summer, let alone 100° with the humidity! I would go back to the YMCA to do personal training lessons. Late in the evening, I would go the local ice rink to do skating lessons and referee hockey. Finally, at 11:00 p.m., I'd get home. I was beyond tired and severely underpaid. I knew that working from 4:45 a.m. until 11:00 p.m. and being broke was not what I wanted to do for the rest of my life. Not to mention I had a brand-new baby on the way, and I didn't want to spend my last free days without children working all the time.

One day, I was talking to my father-in-law, and he asked me, what I was going to do for a job. I told him I wasn't sure. I think that worried him a bit because our family was going to grow soon, and I'm sure he was wondering how I was going to support his daughter and new grandchild. He asked me if I had ever thought about getting into the insurance business. I said, "No." I was thinking to myself, *I don't even like insurance.*

"Well, I can get you an interview with the insurance company I'm working with now."

My dad had always taught me that beggars can't be choosers, so I decided to take the interview. My father-in-law had done very well in the business, so I thought that maybe I could do as well as he had.

While I was going through the three-week interview process with the insurance company, I decided to go to a job placement agency to see if I could get a temporary job. I wanted desperately to be able to work normal business hours during my last free days before my first child was born. I told the lady at the job placement agency I needed a temporary job that I could do while I was trying to get hired on with this insurance company. She asked me, "What do you really want to do for a job?"

I told her that I really wanted to be a stock broker, but I already had a job lined up. I just needed to find a temporary job until the insurance company hired me. She told me that they did permanent placements and they could find me a permanent job. I was persistent, and I told her all I needed was something that I could work normal business hours for the next three weeks until I was hired on with the insurance company.

The lady that owned that job placement agency overheard our conversation. Curious, she flew out of her office and asked me, "Why are you thinking about getting into the insurance business? You know, that's a tough business, and you're not from around here. You really ought to consider doing something else. You're from the north and this is the South. How do you think you're going to make it? You have no friends and no family here you can write business on."

I suppose I could have written all my father-in-law's clients, but Christmas and Thanksgiving would not have been very fun. She continued, "You might want to consider doing something else. Why don't you call my son? He's been in the business for ten years, and he can give you the good, the bad, and the ugly. Then you can decide if you really want to do this."

I proceeded to call him and started to hear a recurring theme from everyone that I talked to about the industry. He told me, "You must work hard early on. If you do, then you'll have the freedom and flexibility to do what you want in the future. You'll also have a great residual income."

I told him I'm working from 4:45 a.m. to 11:00 p.m. at night. I am not afraid of hard work.

He then proceeded to tell me he was not qualified to determine if it was a fit for me. So he recommended that I go talk to the managing partner at New York Life, one of the largest mutual insurance companies in the world.

When I met Steve Adkins, the managing partner at New York Life, and I had an opportunity to spend some time with him in the interview process, I quickly learned that he was somebody that I believed could **lead me to a better future**. He is still, to this day, one of the wisest people I have ever met in my life.

After meeting with Steve I decided to take the job with New York Life. The day I was scheduled to start training on was July 14, 2002—the day my first son, Jake, was born. I had to call in that day to tell them that my wife was having a baby. I jokingly mentioned that I couldn't come to work that day because if I missed the birth of my first child, I would probably need some of the products they sold. My wife would have killed me for missing that day.

I officially started working September 8, 2002. The first three months of my career weren't bad, and the next three months were not so good. I had run out of the few names that I did have and was starting to struggle.

In March of 2003, I went home and sat at the kitchen table with my wife in our two-bedroom house. She said, "Things aren't working out the way we thought they would. You need to get another job, go back to school, or figure something out because we're broke. We have to take out loans to pay our bills. We have a six-month-old baby to feed. If you don't fix this soon, I'm going to leave with Jake and move to Amory with my parents."

Our money problems were causing us to experience **a lot of fear, anxiety, and stress**.

"What am I going to do? I don't have a college degree and I

would make less money building houses. Besides, I'm helping people. I am making a difference in people's lives," I told her.

She cried out, "I don't care! You're not making a difference in our lives!"

I replied, "Point taken."

I told her I would go talk to the managing partner Steve in the morning to see what my options were.

THE TURNING POINT

I walked into Steve's office the next morning.

"Steve, I am grateful for the opportunity I have been given here. I don't mean to sound ungrateful, but I am **not making the kind of money I need to make** to be able to stay here. If something doesn't change soon, I'm afraid I won't be working here much longer."

Steve was an old school teacher and liked to ask a lot of questions to help teach a lesson. He used to say to me, "**It always sounds better coming out of their mouth than it does yours.**" In other words, it's better if you come up with the solution on your own. That way it's your idea and you have to buy in.

So he asked me, "What have you been doing?"

I told him a little bit of this and a little bit of that.

"Have you been following the business plan that has been laid out for 157 years?"

"No, not really."

He then asked me a very important question, "**Do you think you can do this?**"

"Yes, I know I can do this. I just need you to show me what to do. I'm desperate. I have got to make this work or my wife is going to leave me and take my six-month-old son."

"Okay, here is what I want you to do. I want you to **commit to following the business plan for the next thirty days**. Not thirty years, not thirty months. Just thirty days. At the end of thirty days, if you still don't think you can do this, then you can continue to work here. At that point, I'll help you find another job."

"Great! Now I can go home and tell my wife to leave me alone for at least thirty days!"

I learned one of the most important lessons of my life that day. Sometimes you must have somebody believe in you more than you believe in yourself, so you can believe in yourself again. Steve did that for me. Thanks Steve.

When I walked out of Steve's office that day, I wasn't sure if I was going to make it. Nonetheless, I had **decided** that I was going to give it everything I had and do my best. If my best was not good enough, at least I would have done everything I could to make it work. **Do my best and let God take care of the rest** were the only words that kept running through my head.

FROM BROKE TO A SIX-FIGURE INCOME

Thirty days later, I won Agent of the Month! That year I won New Agent of the Year and won the Paid Life Case Leader Award. I made the Million-Dollar Round Table and was number one in the world in term sales in the company. I went from being broke to earning a six-figure income.

When I tell people my story, people ask me all the time, "What changed for you?"

To put it simply, **I made a committed decision to become the person I knew I was capable of becoming because I was tired of being the person I was.** Then I kept making that decision every second, every minute, every hour, and every day from there on out.

Quite often we must have a conversation with ourselves using our own wisdom, knowledge, and experiences to make judgment calls and to rescue ourselves from our own circumstances. We are the only ones that can do that.

I had to use all my wisdom, knowledge, experience, and other people's experiences to decide about the future. Everything I had learned to that point led me to the conclusion that if I did not change, I would have lost everything that was near and dear to me. That is why I decided to change. **I became uncomfortable.**

What will you change in your life to become who you know you can become?

Maybe a doctor has told you that if you don't improve your health, you won't be here to watch your children or grandchildren grow up.

Maybe your spouse or significant other has told you they're going to leave you if you don't change.

Is it that you feel like you have no control over your life?

Is it that you're tired of living paycheck to paycheck and owing people money?

Is it that your children are getting older and this is your last chance to spend time with them while they're young?

Is it that you're afraid that if you die you won't go to heaven?

Is it that you're tired of having no energy and time to do the things you love to do?

Is it that you're dissatisfied with your appearance?

Is it that you're afraid of losing your job?

What are you afraid of?

Whatever it is for you, **if you don't become aware of what is holding you back, you will never get ahead**. You will be trapped in a life of mediocrity with no hope for a better future.

So how do you become aware and start to care?

Awareness starts with recognizing where you've been in the

past, how you ended up where you are in the present, and what your current course for the future is. We will examine this later.

Caring starts with knowing and understanding the benefits of making a committed decision and the consequences of not acting to progress towards your ideal future.

In life, we are temporarily motivated by fear and pain and inspired by ambition, desire, passion, and love.

Motivation and inspiration start with thought. How you think effects everything about you. The conversations we have with ourselves determine what we choose to do. **The most powerful motivational speaker you will ever hear in your life is *you*.** Nobody has more consistent influence over you than you. You are the only person that has the power to change you.

As Deepak Chopra says, "Your feelings are not someone else's fault." Becoming the true you starts with taking responsibility for the internal conversations in your head. **Once you master your mind, you will master your life.**

The secret to turning stress and mess into success is by deciding to change your life, which is usually caused by fear, frustration, anxiety, stress, or guilt. Once these feelings become strong enough, you will change. Remember this though, **if nothing changes, nothing will change**. So welcome adversity because the more pain you experience, the more you will be motivated to change.

I made a committed decision to become the person I knew I was capable of becoming because I was tired of being the person I was.

CHAPTER KEY POINTS:

1. Sometimes you must have somebody believe in you more than you believe in yourself, so you can believe in yourself again.

2. Do your best and let God take care of the rest.

3. Make the right choice every second, every minute, every hour, and every day, because it always impacts the trajectory of your life.

4. Quite often we must have a conversation with ourselves using our wisdom, knowledge, and experience to make judgment calls to rescue ourselves from our own circumstances.

5. In life, we are temporarily motivated by fear and pain, and inspired by ambition, desire, passion, and love.

6. If you don't become aware of what is holding you back, you will never get ahead.

7. The most powerful motivational speaker you will ever hear in your life is you.

8. Once you master your mind, you will master your life.

9. The secret to turning stress and mess into success is by deciding to change your life.

10. If nothing changes, nothing will change.

"Fear is not real. The only place that fear can exist is in our thoughts of the future. It is a product of our imagination, causing us to fear things that do not at present and may not ever exist. That is near insanity. Do not misunderstand me, danger is very real, but fear is a choice."

—WILL SMITH, *AFTER EARTH*

CHAPTER 2

Does Anyone Know Who I Am?

"WHO ARE *YOU*?" SAID THE CATERPILLAR.

THIS WAS NOT AN ENCOURAGING OPENING FOR A CONVERSATION. ALICE REPLIED, RATHER SHYLY, "I—I HARDLY KNOW, SIR, JUST AT PRESENT—AT LEAST I KNOW WHO I *WAS* WHEN I GOT UP THIS MORNING, BUT I THINK I MUST HAVE BEEN CHANGED SEVERAL TIMES SINCE THEN."

—LEWIS CARROLL, *ALICE'S ADVENTURES IN WONDERLAND*

I think a lot of people live life like *Alice in Wonderland*. They wander and are lost without any idea of where they want to get in life while trying to figure out who they really are. I do believe that we change from one season of life to the next just like how Alice said, "I'm never sure what I'm going to be from one minute to another." Have you ever asked yourself, "Who am I?"

I heard a voicemail message one time that said, "Who are you, and what do you want?" Most people spend their whole life trying to figure out those two questions.

When interviewing people, I ask them who they think they truly are. So many people say to me, "You know, nobody has ever really asked me who I truly am. I'm not sure who I am."

That's probably because we're always changing from moment to moment, minute to minute, and season to season within our life.

It stands to reason that we should consistently ask ourselves, "Who am I going to be today?" We play many different roles at different times of our lives. Heck, we play many different roles during the day. Sometimes we are a friend, a colleague, a parent, a teacher, a leader, a follower, a spiritual being, a child, a sibling, an employee, a manager, a coach, a fool, a genius, a failure, or a success. No wonder so many people are confused about who they are! Often the situation or environment we are in determines who we are at that time. At home we are one person and we are another at the office.

The cool thing about free will is that we have been given the power to choose who we are at any given moment in time. Instead of trying to increase comfort or decrease discomfort like most human beings do (because that's what our physical bodies are designed by nature to do), we should use our conscience mind to direct our focus to live out our true purpose in life. **To live out one's true purpose in life, you must decide to follow your conscience versus your habitual rituals that influence the trajectory of your life daily.**

So what is conscience?

Let's look at a couple different views.

Freeman Dyson has suggested a kind of cosmic metaphysics of mind. In his book *Infinite in All Directions*, he writes about three levels of mind: The universe shows evidence of the operations of mind on three levels. The first level is the level of elementary physical processes in quantum mechanics. Matter in quantum mechanics is constantly making choices between alternative possibilities according to probabilistic laws. The second level at which we detect the operations of mind is the level of direct human experience. It is reasonable to believe in the existence of a third level of mind, a mental component of the universe. If we believe in this mental component and call it God, then we can say that we are small pieces of God's mental apparatus.

Conscience, according to Webster's dictionary is *the part of the superego in psychoanalysis that transmits commands and admonitions to the ego.*

Admonitions means *counsel or warning against fault or oversight.*

So who is this voice in your head that is counseling you on whether your actions are morally right or wrong? If this is God speaking to you, whatever you conceive God to be, then what is God trying to tell you?

When you have an internal conversation ask yourself, "Who am I having a conversation with?" Is this God speaking to you or are you speaking to yourself? Can you really have a conversation without including someone else? Who is answering the questions when you ask them? Psychologists would say it is innate knowledge. Christians would say it is infinite wisdom from God which includes:

- omniscience: infinite wisdom
- omnipotence: unlimited power
- omnipresence: present everywhere
- omnibenevolence: perfect goodness

I am not going to profess to be a theologian or psychologist, although I have studied both. However, I think there is truth in the above. I believe we do have conversations with ourselves and sometimes they include God. Have you ever asked yourself, "I wonder what I should eat for supper? Do I really need to buy this?"

You may not have asked God for guidance on those things. That is, you using your innate knowledge. We usually don't ask God the easy questions that guide our daily actions. We usually only ask the questions we don't have the innate knowledge, wisdom, or experience to answer ourselves. Then we turn to God for omniscience, which is infinite wisdom, to get the answer.

The same thing happens when we encounter adversity and pain. If we don't have the strength to overcome the challenge by ourselves, we seek God's omnipotence and faith to help us overcome the challenge at hand.

When we must make an ethical decision, we seek the teachings of religious scriptures based on omnibenevolence. An example of perfect goodness is the way Jesus lived his life. We then make our decision based on what the teacher has taught us, which comes from the perfect goodness.

Aristotle taught that people make decisions in three different ways: logos, pathos, and ethos.

Logos means logic. It speaks to the mind or head and credibility and competency. In relation to your purpose in life, it is the rational reason for acting on a decision. In other words, we believe that the evidence being presented to us is a good reason for us to act. Sometimes this is referred to as deciding with your head or mind.

Pathos means passion or emotion. It speaks to the heart. Of the three, this is said to be the strongest. In relation to your purpose in life, pathos strongly appeals to your faith and fear surrounding decisions you must make. Fear and faith consistently affect decisions we make every day. If you are in sales, you might think to yourself, *If I call this person, they may reject me, and I am fearful of being embarrassed by rejection.* So you may hesitate to make the call. On the other hand, you might think to yourself, *My purpose in life is to reach out and offer my product or service to this person so they can improve the quality of their life.* The fear is overcome by the faith that you will make a difference in that person's life. **Our reason for doing something in life can be driven by the emotions we want to experience at any given moment.** It is important that we **use all our decision-making faculties** so that we **don't end up living an emotionally-driven life instead of a purpose-driven life.**

This is where ethos comes into play. Ethos is ethics, otherwise known as honesty and the truth. What you are seeking when it comes to the purpose of your life is the truth. You must be honest with yourself first and foremost. As they say, the truth will set you free. Once you find your true purpose in life, I believe it creates freedom for you to live your life the way it is designed to be lived. Some people spend their whole life seeking their true purpose. Oftentimes, they get to the end of their life and realize that their true purpose in life was to live life one purposeful day at a time. I am not sure what your individual purpose is, but I believe the universal purpose of all our lives is to live in harmony as one collective group of spirits and beings to enrich the lives of each other.

Can you imagine what the world would be like if we all had the patience, unconditional love, and spiritual wisdom of Jesus, the resilience to endure great suffering like Gandhi, the passion to serve like Mother Theresa, and the trust that we all had each other's best interest at heart?

What is your purpose on Earth at this moment? As Shakespeare writes in his famous quote from *As You Like It,*

"All the world's a stage, and all the men and women merely players. They have their exits and their entrances, and one man in his time plays many parts, his acts being seven ages."

If this is true, I submit to you that you have more than one purpose in life. You have many purposes each day because you are playing many roles each day. You were created for a world that was not created by you, but *for* you. You are meant to be here. If you are a parent, your purpose may be to lead, teach, love, protect, listen, and provide. At other times, you may need to be a friend to someone who needs your help. You might be called on to be an example for someone to learn from. Whatever your calling, your purpose changes from moment to moment depending upon the decisions you make and what you focus on.

Trying to figure out why you are on Earth is not the point. Will you ever fully know why you were put here on Earth? I don't know that you will. I do know that you can choose your purpose and I think the important thing to remember is to choose a purpose that will inspire you to live your life in a way that alleviates suffering and creates residual joy. At the end of your life you will only have memories. I anticipate you will want as many of those memories to be joyful.

Being created with the ability to choose our destiny gives us the power to choose our purpose.

"The two most important days in your life are the day you are born and the day you find out why."

—ANONYMOUS

So the question is: *What is your purpose in life now?*

_____

_____

_____

_____

_____

_____

_____

_____

_____

_____

_____

_____

_____

_____

_____

_____

_____

_____

_____

_____

_____

_____

_____

_____

CHAPTER KEY POINTS:

1. Our reason for doing something in life can be driven by the emotions we want to experience at any given moment.

2. It is important that we use all our decision-making faculties so that we don't end up living an emotionally-driven life instead of a purpose-driven life.

3. To live out one's true purpose in life, you must decide to follow your conscience versus your habitual rituals that influence the trajectory of your life daily.

4. You were created by a world that was not created by you, but *for* you. You are meant to be here.

5. Being created with the ability to choose our destiny gives us the power to choose our purpose.

CHAPTER 3

Who are You Going to Be?

> "I WONDER IF I'VE BEEN CHANGED IN THE NIGHT? LET ME THINK: WAS I THE SAME WHEN I GOT UP THIS MORNING? I ALMOST THINK I CAN REMEMBER FEELING A LITTLE DIFFERENT. BUT IF I'M NOT THE SAME, THE NEXT QUESTION IS, WHO IN THE WORLD AM I? AH, *THAT'S* THE GREAT PUZZLE!"
>
> —LEWIS CARROLL, *ALICE'S ADVENTURES IN WONDERLAND*

I think so many people struggle with their identity because they don't recognize who they are to be at any given moment in time. To be always starts with the focus of your mind.

Being begins with seeing. You must see what you want to become. Your thoughts determine your actions and your actions ultimately determine who you are or become. **The reason why you are the person you are today is because of the decisions you made about acting or not acting in the past.** Your career or profession is what it is today because of the decisions you have made at work daily. Your body is the way it is today because of decisions you have made in the past about exercise, the food you put into your body, and your sleeping habits. Your bank account has the amount of money in it today because of the decisions you have made in the past about spending and saving. Your marriage or relationships are good or bad today because of the decisions you have made in the past about how much time you devoted to making them the way you want them.

If your success in life is largely determined by the decisions you make daily, then it stands to reason that we should **make smarter decisions every day**. Pretty simple, right? Easier said than done. All decisions start in your mind and are **influenced by your focus at the time you make the decision**. Because of limiting habits, limiting beliefs, and other external factors, it is imperative that we control the focus of our mind. If we don't, someone or something else will.

"If you don't design your own life plan, chances are you'll fall into someone else's plan. And guess what they have planned for you? Not much."

—JIM ROHN

Let's say for example you want to be a **millionaire**. You must do what it takes to be a **millionaire**. **Millionaires** are **millionaires because they take specific actions** that create the wealth they want and need to become **millionaires**. So why do **millionaires** take the specific actions to become **millionaires**? Because their mind is programmed to think like a **millionaire**. I then ask, "Why do **millionaires** think like **millionaires**?" Because at some point in their life, they saw what a **millionaire's** life was like. They wanted to become like that person because they associated happiness with being a **millionaire or pain with not being a millionaire**. What is it that you want to be? After reading this paragraph you may be thinking of becoming a **millionaire** because of the amount of times I said **millionaire**. See how your focus can be shifted?

If focus is so important, then **how do you control the focus of your mind**? One way is by reading. When you read, your mind is focused on the words on the page which manifest in your mind and creates thoughts. The other way is through questioning and visualization.

René Descartes, the father of modern philosophy, theorized that when we think, we become. For example, if you think you are, **in your mind** you are whatever you think you are at that moment. What you believe to be true is true to you. **Belief is stronger than fact or truth.**

When we are told repeatedly that we are either good at something or not good at something, we can start to believe that to be true, which consequently influences our performance. A great example of this is with kids. We start to label them as a good student, athlete, or something else. They start to believe that about themselves.

If we tell them that enough, they eventually start to become that person. Most of this is done through unintentional conditioning. A lot of times we do it through questioning. This is more powerful than telling someone because they must answer the question in their own mind and in their own voice. When a question is asked to us, our brain is designed to answer. **Questioning is the most powerful way to shift someone's focus.** The question forces us to think about the answer in our mind, therefore shifting our focus. When you question someone's ability repeatedly it plants seeds of doubt in their brain. **For me to have faith, my belief must be stronger than your doubt.**

Examples of this are:

A parent says to their child, "You **never** listen to me. Why can't you do what I tell you to do?"

The child's brain searches for an answer to the question. The brain pulls the answer from a bank of experiences in the child's mind. This is usually the most recent experience, which would be them not listening. Because the parent just asked that question, the child thinks *I am not a good listener.*

For someone like a spouse, who has a larger bank of experiences, questioning them creates doubt in their mind. Even if they are confident in who they are, this can lead to uncertainty. When other people question us, our brain starts asking "Why are they questioning me? Something must be wrong."

A manager says to an employee, "Why are you **always** late?"

At that moment, the employee thinks, *I am always late.* This may not even be entirely true.

A coach says to an athlete, "Why aren't you giving 100%?"

The athlete thinks, *I am not giving 100%.*

Even though the coach's intentions are to motivate, a seed has been planted in the player's head that can create doubt.

When someone says, "You are always late," or "You never listen," we start to believe what we hear consistently. If someone else sees us that way, we question our own identity.

This happens in abusive relationships where one spouse overpowers the other by saying things like, "If you leave me, you will never find anyone as good as me," or "Who would want to be with someone like you?" When messages like this are communicated to people with weak belief systems at high emotional levels, it can be very detrimental to one's self esteem. **We want to plant seeds of confidence, not fear or doubt.**

If we are not careful, these questions can become a self-fulfilling prophecy. When someone else sees us as failing to do something, it creates doubt in our minds and shakes our confidence. This is especially true if it is someone that we trust and look up to. Quite often we use the words *always* and *never* in our conversations. I believe the only time we should use these two words are in these contexts: to use these words in this mantra, "**Always do your best and never give up!**"

On the flipside, the great news is we can use this to strengthen positive beliefs as well. **Eventually over time, our beliefs are shaped by our experiences. These can be real or imagined.** If I consistently tell someone that they are great at something and that I believe in them, eventually they will start to believe it. They will believe in themselves. If you don't believe me, try it. What's the worst thing that could happen? You will make somebody's day by saying some nice things about them. The best time to do this is when you catch someone doing something good. The most recent experience in their mind is going to support what you're saying.

Now that you recognize how the psychology of focus determines your success, you can use it to get immediate results anytime you want.

How can you apply this principle to your life now to get better results instantly?

Read books, articles, quotes, and anything you can get your hands on that will support your beliefs. Use visualization to imagine your ideal outcome. Use questions to control the focus of your mind.

Quick and easy implementation:

Answer the following questions in three minutes or less. Write the first thing that comes to your mind.

Write down the top three things you *think* people would say about you if you were not around.

1. _____

2. _____

3. _____

Now write down the top three things you *want* people to say about you.

Examples:

I make people happier with my sense of humor.

I raise kids that respect others and themselves.

I am a unique individual who makes other people's lives better.

1. _____

2. _____

3. _____

Ask someone close to you what they think you are most passionate about.

Examples:

I love serving people.

I am loyal.

I love my kids.

1. _____

2. _____

3. _____

Write down three things you want people to feel after being around you.

Examples:

Residual joy

Confidence

Being heard

1. _____

2. _____

3. _____

Who do you really want to be?

_____

_____

_____

_____

_____

_____

_____

_____

_____

_____

CHAPTER KEY NOTES

1. Questioning is the most powerful way to shift your focus.

2. For me to have faith, my belief must be stronger than your doubt.

3. Always do you best and never give up! This sounds simple, but if you do it your life will be better.

4. Belief is stronger than fact or truth.

5. Eventually, we become what we think about the most.

6. Being begins with seeing.

7. The reason why you are the person you are today is because of the decisions you made about acting or not acting in the past.

"We become what we want to be by consistently being what we want to become each day."

—RICHARD G. SCOTT

CHAPTER 4

I Think, I Am

"I THINK, THEREFORE I AM."

—RENÉ DESCARTES

I Am conditioning is all about the conversations we have with ourselves. One of my favorite authors Susan Scott says, "We are always having conversations with ourselves and sometimes they include other people."

These conversations are most effective when we speak in present tense as if the thing we are trying to accomplish is already occurring at that very moment. For example, if I want to be a great athlete, I will say, "I am a great athlete." I am speaking it into reality.

If I also act like a great athlete and do what a great athlete does, then inevitably I become a great athlete even if only for a moment. The trick is to keep thinking, acting, and doing what great athletes do.

In all my years of playing and coaching sports, I have discovered **the secret to winning.** It is momentum and focus. Almost every game is won or lost because of momentum. Almost all momentum starts with laser-like focus of the mind on getting the job done at that very moment. Athletes are always talking to themselves, whether it is a tennis player about to serve a ball, a hockey player about to take a penalty shot, or a basketball player shooting a free throw. In every sport, the games are won or lost in the heads of the athlete.

Well, guess what? Your life is the same way. It is won or lost in your mind. You must control your focus if you want to win the game of life.

In the pages that follow, I am going to give you a technique that you can use daily to get the results you desire. It will change the momentum of your life by controlling your focus.

Here is what I want you to do right **NOW** so you can start seeing a **transformation instantly. Read the instructions and then act.**

MOTIVATIONAL NOTE:
MOST BOOKS DON'T STOP YOU IN THE MIDDLE AND MAKE YOU ACT. THAT'S WHY MOST PEOPLE DON'T GET RESULTS FROM BOOKS THEY READ. SO BE SURE TO DO THIS NOW AND YOU CAN THANK ME LATER.

1. First read the sample of the *I Am* statement I have provided for you in the different roles of one's life.

2. Clear your mind of all preconceived notions that might obscure the truth. You want to start with a blank slate.

3. Write your own personalized *I Am* statement for each important role that you play in each area of your life: personally, professionally, financially, and spiritually.

4. At the bottom of your statement, list three questions that you will repeatedly ask yourself daily to control your focus on or list three action steps you will take today to propel you toward your goals.

5. Now post these statements in a place where you will see them every day to control your focus. You may want to put your spiritual statement on your bedside table, your personal statements in the kitchen or on your bathroom mirror, and your professional statement in your car and in your office.

6. Set an alarm on your phone or calendar to go off at the same time each day to prompt you to read your *Focus Formula*. This will become a ritual.

7. The most important question you need to answer in life every single day is this: Who will I be today?

Who we become is determined by the questions we ask ourselves from moment to moment and the decisions we make and the actions we take.

Ask yourself better questions to make better decisions and you will get better results.

"Employ your courage when making decisions so that you reap the benefits of good judgement and not the consequences of inaction."

—Dave Jesiolowski

PROFESSION

The first area of your life that we will define and declare who you are to be is in your professional life.

Being great in your profession starts by discovering your obsession.

When I say obsession, I don't mean work all the time and never spend time doing anything you enjoy. What I mean is finding out what you love to do. Do it so well that you don't have to do it as much because you are making so much money.

Answer the questions below to gain clarity around what you love to do.

On a scale of 1 to 10, how happy are you in your current profession? Circle the number:

1   2   3   4   5   6   7   8   9   10

Do you love what you currently do?

□   Yes

□   No

Is it your passion?

□   Yes

□   No

Where does your knowledge, talent, and obsession intersect? (i.e., What do you spend most of your time, money, and energy on?)

- ☐ Entrepreneurship: Building the future
- ☐ Personal Development: Reading, writing, coaching other people
- ☐ Leadership: Inspiring and coaching people
- ☐ Examination: Analyzing people or data
- ☐ Service: Serving people
- ☐ Management: Directing people or systems
- ☐ Relationships: Interacting with people
- ☐ Operations: Organizing, fixing, collaborating
- ☐ Administration: Processing, following through
- ☐ Solving Problems: Vision, strategy, or execution

What are you amazing at?

_____

When you were growing up, what did you dream of becoming?

_____

What makes you happy?

_____

What are your hobbies?

_____

What are you good at or want to be good at?

_____

What is one word that describes the person you want to be professionally?

_____

Describe what a perfect day would look like in your life. What time do you wake up? What time do you go to sleep? Do you exercise? What do you eat? Who do you spend time with? Where do you go? How do you want to spend your time? What emotions do you experience? How much money do you earn? Be honest with yourself here.

_____

_____

_____

_____

What professional accomplishment are you most proud of in your life so far?

_____

What would the perfect headline of your professional autobiography say about you right now?

_____

If you were writing your professional obituary, what would the perfect headline say?

_____

What's missing in your professional life?

_____

If you died yesterday, what would you regret not having done in your professional life?

_____

_____

List anybody that is currently contaminating or limiting your progress.

_____

_____

_____

List anybody that is currently contributing to your progress.

_____

_____

_____

Now create your own Professional *Focus Formulas*.

Example:

I Am **P**assionate because I believe in what I do

I Am **R**eliable because I am disciplined

I Am **O**utworking my competitors every day

I Am **F**earless because I control my actions

I Am **F**aithful because I am confident in my abilities

I Am **E**nriching other people's lives

I Am **S**ucceeding one day at a time

I Am **S**killed in communication

I Am **I**nspiring others to act

I Am **O**utstanding at building relationships

I Am **N**ever fearful of the unknown

I Am **A**ccomplishing all my goals, dreams, and desires

I Am **L**earning to be the best I can be

I Am a Professional

Example Focus Questions:

1. What is the most important use of my time right now?

2. For today to be a great day, what must I accomplish?

3. Why must I accomplish these things?

Write your own *I Am A Professional Focus Formula* and focus questions.

I Am _____

I Am _____

I Am _____

I Am _____

I Am _____

I Am a Professional

Have a healthy obsession for your profession.

Your Focus Questions:

1. _____
_____?

2. _____
_____?

3. _____
_____?

Action rewards you with results. Results = Freedom.

PARENTING

The next area of your life that we will define and declare who you are to be is in parenting. If you are not a parent, then you can skip this section. If you are a parent, this could be the most important role you will ever play in your life.

Being able to influence who your children become is an amazing opportunity to impact the world. If you do a great job your child will be your legacy that lives on beyond your life. If you do a poor job, then the consequences can be devastating.

Not only do we have to make decisions on how we are going to lead, teach, coach, motivate, inspire, and demonstrate how to be responsible, reliable, trustworthy human beings, we must make decisions for them that can change the course of their future.

We as parents ultimately have the power to alter our children's definitions of themselves and the world. This is a revelation that we must own and be proactive vs. reactive with amid the daily challenges of life.

Unveiling this truth has helped me realize that **being a parent can be the most challenging season of our lives as well as the most rewarding.** Children change so much from birth to adulthood that there isn't any other season of life like it. Transformation is happening more rapidly in the structure and chemistry of the body and the development of their mind during childhood than any other point in our lives.

I remember a funny story from when my son Jake was three years old. I was trying to teach him responsibility from a young age by telling him that his job was to take out the trash. He was sitting at the kitchen island while my wife was making cookies and he expressed with a great amount of confidence that his job was to eat cookies.

That's what I get for trying to instill responsibility in a three-year-old.

Our job is to teach our children that happiness can be achieved by accepting responsibility for oneself, just make sure you know when to instill that responsibility.

Once our children understand that they have the power to choose how they respond to events, environments, or circumstances that they are faced with in life, they will truly understand the secret to being happy.

Being focused in this area can be particularly challenging because it requires a lot of energy to raise children. Things like exercise, eating right, and getting the ideal amount of rest may sound like trivial things, but over time they can impact your ability to focus and make good parenting decisions. So remember to use this Focus Formula along with a schedule or routine that will put you in a position to be the best parent possible.

That might mean sitting down one day a week and planning so you are ready for the daily challenges of parenting.

Examples for fathers:

I Am **G**rateful for my family

I Am **R**esponsible to my children

I Am **E**ncouraging when times are tough

I Am **A** teacher, leader, and coach

I Am **T**rustworthy

I Am **D**ependable

I Am **A**ccountable

I Am **D**etermined

I Am a Great Dad

Example Focus Questions:

1. Why did I become a dad?

2. How much quality time will I spend with my children today?

3. What will I teach my children today that will improve the quality of their life now and in the future?

"PARENTHOOD IS THE MOST IMPORTANT LEADERSHIP RESPONSIBILITY IN LIFE AND WILL PROVIDE THE GREATEST LEVELS OF HAPPINESS AND JOY. AND WHEN TRUE LEADERSHIP—I.E., VISION, DISCIPLINE, PASSION, AND CONSCIENCE—IS NOT MANIFESTED IN PARENTHOOD, IT WILL PROVIDE THE GREATEST SOURCE OF SORROW AND DISAPPOINTMENT."

—STEPHEN COVEY,
THE 8TH HABIT: FROM EFFECTIVENESS TO GREATNESS

Write your own *I Am A Great Dad Focus Formula* and focus questions.

I Am _____

I Am _____

I Am _____

I Am _____

I Am _____

I Am a Great Dad

Focus Questions:

1. _____
_____?

2. _____
_____?

3. _____
_____?

Action rewards you with results. Results = Freedom.

Examples for mothers:

I Am **G**rateful and love my family unconditionally

I Am **R**esilient

I Am **E**mpathic, always

I Am **A** kind, loving, giving, beautiful woman

I Am **T**rustworthy and honest

I Am **M**ade to love

I Am **O**rganized

I Am **M**ulti-Talented

I Am a Great Mom

Example Focus Questions:

1. Why did I become a mother?

2. How can I be consistent in the discipline of my children?

3. How will I love my children unconditionally today?

"THE MOMENT A CHILD IS BORN, THE MOTHER IS ALSO BORN. SHE NEVER EXISTED BEFORE. THE WOMAN EXISTED BUT THE MOTHER, NEVER. A MOTHER IS SOMETHING ABSOLUTELY NEW."

—OSHSO

Write your *I Am A Great Mom Focus Formula* and focus questions.

I Am _____

I Am _____

I Am _____

I Am _____

I Am _____

I Am a Great Mom

Focus Questions:

1. _____
_____?

2. _____
_____?

3. _____
_____?

Action rewards you with results. Results = Freedom.

Example for grandparents:

I Am **G**iving

I Am **R**esponsible for passing on my legacy

I Am **A**dmired by my grandkids

I Am **N**eeded to provide wisdom about life

I Am **D**evoted to my family

I Am **P**atient because of my wisdom

I Am **A**llowed to spoil my grandchildren

I Am **R**espected

I Am **E**xperienced

I Am **N**oble

I Am **T**rustworthy

I Am a Grandparent

Example Focus Questions:

1. What lessons will I share with my grandchildren?

2. How much time will I spend with my grandchildren this week?

3. What is something important to my grandchildren that I can do with them?

Write down your own *I Am A Grandparent Focus Formula* and focus questions.

I Am   _____

I Am   _____

I Am   _____

I Am   _____

I Am   _____

I Am a Grandparent

Focus Questions:

1. _____
   _____?

2. _____
   _____?

3. _____
   _____?

Action rewards you with results. Results = Freedom.

FINANCIAL FREEDOM AND INDEPENDENCE

Having been a financial planner with two Fortune 500 companies for the last fifteen years, I have worked with many millionaires. I am about to share with you the top twenty-five secrets they have used to have financial freedom.

What is financial freedom and independence? And what can it do for you?

Financial freedom and independence is being able to do what you want because your income exceeds your expenses.

Having financial freedom gives you the ability to live life on your terms, have a great quality of life, freedom to spend your time how you want, and the confidence to take risks to follow your dreams.

Top twenty-five secrets to financial success:

1. Choose a career that you love and that solves a problem for other people.

2. Invest your time in revenue-producing activities.

3. Save every month (20% or more).

4. Schedule your days diligently.

5. Act consistently every day.

6. Make good decisions with your finances.

7. Leverage your time and talents.

8. Delegate things you aren't good at.

9. Find your niche to become rich. Discover what other people want and provide it to them.

10. Focus on actions that create wealth.

11. Study the following: compound interest, debt reduction, taxes, savings tips, investing, and diversification.

12. Take calculated risks.

13. **Break your lifestyle addiction.**

14. Invest in good people to work for you.

15. Invest in self-development.

16. Be analytical.

17. Leverage and manage debt wisely.

18. Track where you spend your money (expenses, tax deductions, etc.).

19. Have a diversified investment strategy. Many of the top millionaires I have worked with employed this strategy to build their wealth.

20. Don't be an emotional investor or make emotional decisions with your money.

21. Hire the best money advisors you can afford and that you trust. They will pay for themselves.

22. Be disciplined enough to follow the plan.

23. Hire a business coach.

24. Don't lose money.

25. **The rate of savings is more important than the rate of return.**

Achieving financial freedom comes down to making better decisions with your money. It takes time to become wealthy so be patient and consistent.

Score yourself on a scale of 1–5 in each of the following:

1. I have a career I love and that solves a problem for other people.

1   2   3   4   5

2. I invest my time in revenue-producing activities.

1   2   3   4   5

3. I save every month. At least 20% or more.

1   2   3   4   5

4. I schedule my days diligently.

1   2   3   4   5

5. I act consistently every day.

1   2   3   4   5

6. I make good decisions with my finances.

1   2   3   4   5

7. I leverage my time and talents.

1   2   3   4   5

8. I delegate things I am not good at.

1   2   3   4   5

9. I have found a niche that gives other people what they want and I provide it to them.

1   2   3   4   5

10. I focus on actions that create wealth.

1   2   3   4   5

11. I study compound interest, debt reduction, taxes, savings tips, investing, and diversification.

1   2   3   4   5

12. I take calculated risks.

1   2   3   4   5

13. I am not addicted to an expensive lifestyle.

1   2   3   4   5

14. I invest in good people to work for me or work around good people.

1   2   3   4   5

15. I invest in self-development.

1   2   3   4   5

16. I analyze my decisions surrounding money.

1   2   3   4   5

17. I leverage and manage debt wisely.

1   2   3   4   5

18. I track where I spend my money.

1   2   3   4   5

19. I have a diversified investment strategy.

1   2   3   4   5

20. I control my emotions when investing.

1   2   3   4   5

21. I hire the best money advisors I can afford and whom I trust.

1   2   3   4   5

22. I am disciplined enough and follow my financial plan.

1   2   3   4   5

23. I have financial mentors in my life.

1   2   3   4   5

24. I don't lose money.

1   2   3   4   5

25. I rely more on saving than on the rate of return to ensure my financial future.

1   2   3   4   5

Now go back and look at the areas that you scored less than three in and ask yourself what will you do to improve in each of those areas? You may want to include some of these in your focus questions.

Sample questions could include:

- Have I tracked where I am spending my money today?
- How will I delegate things that I am not good at or need someone else to do? My time can be spent on things that I am genius at.
- Am I exercising discipline with my spending habits?
- How will I focus on actions that create wealth for me today?
- Do I have my day scheduled so I will be as efficient as possible today?

Example for financial freedom:

I Am earning $1,000,000 per year

I Am saving 20% of my income every month

I Am debt free

I Am worth $10,000,000

I Am on track to retire at 55

I Am a multi-millionaire

I Am generating multiple streams of income

I Am enjoying financial freedom and do the things I enjoy without worrying about money

I Am managing risk effectively

I Am a learner, which makes me an earner

I Am smart with my money

I Am Financially Independent

Example Focus Questions:

1. How will I save money today?

2. How will I generate additional income today?

3. What will I do today to increase my net worth?

Write your *I Am Financially Independent Focus Formula* and focus questions.

I Am _____

I Am _____

I Am _____

I Am _____

I Am _____

I Am _____

I Am _____

I Am Financially Independent

Focus Questions:

1. _____
   _____?

2. _____
   _____?

3. _____
   _____?

Action rewards you with results. Results = Freedom.

HEALTH

When it comes to being the best version of yourself in life and business, your health is vital to your success. If you don't get enough sleep, that can cause stress. If you don't exercise, you can become overweight. If you eat poorly, you can contract disease and become obese. If you don't meditate, your mind becomes stressed. If you don't pray, you miss out on the omniscience (infinite Wisdom), omnipotence (unlimited power), omnipresence (present everywhere), and omnibenevolence (perfect goodness) that a holy spirit can provide.

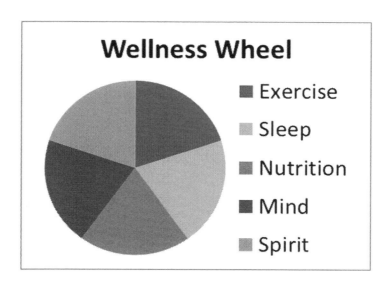

When writing out your formula for optimal health, consider these questions below.

KEYS TO OPTIMAL HEALTH

Body

How many times a week will you exercise?

What will you do to improve your flexibility, agility, balance, strength, power, and endurance?

How can you enjoy your exercise routine more?

What exercises do you love to do?

Nutrition

What will you eat to prevent disease and maintain an optimal body mass index?

How much water will you consume daily?

What foods will you stop eating?

Mind

How will you manage your emotions?

How can you use the power of breath to calm your mind?

How will you stay focused on what matters most?

Spirit

How can you use meditation and prayer to calm your mind?

Sleep

What time will you wake up in the morning?

What time will you go to sleep at night? I have a rule that I turn off all screens after 10:00 p.m., so that I can wind down before bed. (That includes: TV, cell, laptop, iPad, etc.)

What is the optimal temperature for sleeping in your home? Studies say between 60° to 72° Fahrenheit is best.

What will you do thirty minutes before you go to sleep? You might meditate or read.

Every single night, Benjamin Franklin would evaluate his day to see if he was making progress.

Ask yourself, "How could I have made today better?"

Then ask, "What was my best memory of the day?"

Plan the next day. Write notes for tomorrow. Keep a notepad by your bed.

Write in your journal at the end of the day.

Read something inspirational before bed so you plant a seed of positivity that can grow overnight.

Some apps you can download to help you be healthier:

Headspace: Use it to clear your mind at night and get a better night's rest.

My Plate from *Livestrong*: Use this to track your eating. When I was an athlete, we had to track all of our workouts and diet in the summer to make sure we were on track for our goals by the beginning of training camp. Tracking your eating makes you aware of the bad foods that you are eating and helps you make better choices surrounding your diet.

Use *qigong* to cultivate the body's natural energy. See website link below. Lee Holden's seven minutes of magic is the best and easiest program I have used. I do it every morning to kick-start my day. www.excercisetoheal.com

Example for good health:

I Am waking up at 5:30 every morning.

I Am going to sleep before 10:30 every night.

I Am meditating for ten minutes every day.

I Am tracking what I eat at every meal.

I Am drinking eight glasses of water every day.

I Am shutting off all screens by 10:00 p.m.

I Am eating less than 2500 calories per day.

I Am stretching to stay flexible.

I Am exercising daily.

I Am eliminating stress in my life through deep breathing, patience, prayer, laughter, and focusing on the things that I can control.

I Am HEALTHY

Example Focus Questions:

1. What will I eat today to ensure optimal health?

2. How will I prevent myself from becoming stressed?

3. What exercises will I do today?

"THE WAY YOU THINK, THE WAY YOU BEHAVE, THE WAY YOU EAT, CAN INFLUENCE YOUR LIFE BY 30 TO 50 YEARS."

—DEEPAK CHOPRA

Write your *I Am Healthy Focus Formula* and focus questions.

I Am _____

I Am _____

I Am _____

I Am _____

I Am _____

I Am _____

I Am _____

I Am HEALTHY

Focus Questions:

1. _____

_____?

2. _____

_____?

3. _____

_____?

Action rewards you with results. Results = Freedom.

SPIRITUALITY

Example for Christians:

I Am **C**onsistently living a godly life.

I Am **H**ere to be a part of something bigger.

I Am **R**eligiously seeking God's will.

I Am **I**nspiring others to know God.

I Am **S**piritually blessed with God's forgiveness.

I Am **T**rusting God's plan for my life.

I Am **I**nspired to be like Jesus.

I Am **A**ble to overcome temptation.

I Am **N**ot afraid of death because I know I will go to heaven.

I Am a Christian

Example Focus Questions:

1. How will I overcome temptation?

2. How will I give unconditional love, grace, and mercy to someone who doesn't deserve it?

3. Who will I serve?

Write down your own *I Am A Christian Focus Formula* or your own spiritual commitment statement and focus questions.

I Am _____

I Am _____

I Am _____

I Am _____

I Am _____

I Am _____

I Am _____

I Am a _____

Focus Questions:

1. _____
_____?

2. _____
_____?

3. _____
_____?

Action rewards you with results. Results = Freedom.

RELATIONSHIPS

Have you ever wondered why people get married?

Being married or in a committed relationship is not always easy because human beings are born dependent on other human beings. Therefore, we start our lives being programmed that everything will be given to us, which teaches us to be self-centered.

Every problem I have ever seen in relationships has something to do with selfishness. If someone does not get their way, they quite often become disappointed, frustrated, agitated, or angry.

Frustration, anger, and disappointment arise when someone has a perceived resistance to their desires being satisfied. The emotions stem from a failed expectation of a perceived outcome.

For two people to be happy in a committed relationship, some sacrifices need to be made. No two human beings are exactly alike. People do not always agree on everything. This is especially true between a man and a woman. In fact, Israeli researchers have discovered 6,500 genetic differences between the sexes.

Quite often we think our spouses or significant others are always asking us to make sacrifices. They are not the only ones doing that. If you think about it, for any friendship to be successful, you must make sacrifices. Your employer has probably at some point asked you to or will ask you to make sacrifices. It is not just with our spouses or significant others.

It is interesting how we will make sacrifices for our friends but not the person we are supposed to care about more than anyone in the world.

Why is that? I think sometimes we take our spouses or significant others for granted.

Being grateful for your spouse is vital to the success of any relationship.

For one to love another, they must have love within them. You cannot give that which you do not possess.

Let's now write out a vision for how you want your relationship with your spouse or significant other to be.

A great book to improve your relationship is *The Love Dare*.

Spend time studying how to be a better partner and your relationship will grow and be what you want it to be.

Learn to become selfless and communicate better with your spouse or significant other and your relationship will grow and flourish.

Example for wives:

I Am **S**trong

I Am **E**ntrusting

I Am **L**oving

I Am **F**riendly

I Am **L**oyal to my husband

I Am **E**ngaged in our relationship

I Am **S**acrificial

I Am **S**mart and successful

I Am **W**illing to do what it takes to be a great wife

I Am **I**ndependent

I Am **F**aithful

I Am **E**ncouraging

I Am a Selfless Wife

Example Focus Questions:

1. How can I love my husband unconditionally today?

2. What does my husband need from me to feel respected?

3. How will we benefit from me exercising patience, grace, kindness, selflessness, cooperation, and forgiveness?

Write your own *I Am A Selfless Wife Focus Formula* and focus questions.

I Am _____

I Am _____

I Am _____

I Am _____

I Am _____

I Am _____

I Am _____

I Am a Selfless Wife

Focus Questions:

1. _____
_____?

2. _____
_____?

3. _____
_____?

Action rewards you with results. Results = Freedom.

Example for husbands:

I Am **L**oving

I Am **O**ne with my wife

I Am **V**ery grateful for my wife

I Am **I**nspiring

I Am **N**oble

I Am **G**rateful

I Am **H**onest

I Am **U**nderstanding

I Am **S**weet to my wife

I Am **B**rave

I Am **A**ccountable

I Am **N**ot selfish

I Am **D**evoted

I Am a Loving Husband

Example Focus Questions:

1. How can I love my wife unconditionally today?

2. What does my wife need from me to feel loved?

3. How will we benefit from me exercising patience, kindness, selflessness, cooperation, and forgiveness?

Write your own *I Am A Loving Husband Focus Formula* and focus questions.

I Am _____

I Am _____

I Am _____

I Am _____

I Am _____

I Am _____

I Am _____

I Am a Loving Husband

Focus Questions:

1. _____
_____?

2. _____
_____?

3. _____
_____?

Action rewards you with results. Results = Freedom.

You may ask, "What does this have to do with outperforming myself and driving results?"

The answer is everything.

Everything in your life has a cause and effect. If you are experiencing turmoil at home, it will eventually bleed into your professional life or vice versa. **Any area of your life can affect any other area of your life at any given moment in time.**

"Today you are you! That is truer than true! There is no one alive who is you-er than you!"

—Dr. Seuss,
Happy Birthday to You

CHAPTER KEY NOTES

1. *I Am* conditioning is all about the conversations we have with ourselves.

2. Being great in your profession starts by discovering your obsession.

3. Our job is to teach our children that happiness can be achieved by accepting responsibility for oneself.

4. *We as parents ultimately have the power to alter our children's definitions of themselves and the world. This is a revelation that we must own and be proactive vs. reactive with amid the daily challenges of life.*

5. Who we become is determined by the questions we ask ourselves from moment to moment along with the decisions we make and the actions we take.

6. Break your lifestyle addiction.

7. The rate of savings is more important than the rate of return.

8. When it comes to being the best version of yourself in life and business, your health is vital to your success.

9. Every problem I have ever seen in relationships has something to do with selfishness.

10. For one to love another, they must have love within them. You cannot give that which you do not possess.

11. Any area of your life can affect any other area of your life at any given moment in time.

"Lord, we know what we are, but know not what we may be."

—WILLIAM SHAKESPEARE, *HAMLET*

CHAPTER 5

Make Money to Make a Difference: Success and Significance Lists

"WE MAKE A LIVING BY WHAT WE GET, BUT WE MAKE A LIFE BY WHAT WE GIVE."

—WINSTON CHURCHILL

Now let's tie all this together and put this into action. You need to make a **Success List** and a **Significance List** of things to do every day. A Success List is all the essential things you must do every day to **be successful**. Most people attribute being successful to making a certain level of income, but there are other things to consider. By creating this list, you should eliminate all things from your life that you don't need to do. Only list the key activities in each area of your life that will ensure your success. A success list looks something like this:

Your success list can contain the following: health, wealth, and your profession.

Health pertains to your mind, body, and spirit.

Wealth pertains to your financial security, financial freedom, or financial abundance.

Your profession pertains to your performance in your career. These are essential to living a successful life.

Success List: Actions I take every day to be successful.

Success List Examples:

Mind:

- ☐ Ask yourself focus questions that will enhance the quality of your life. See your questions at the end of each *I Am Focus Formula*.

- ☐ I sleep ___ hours (7 hours)

- ☐ I meditate for ___ minutes (10 minutes)

- ☐ I exercise for ___ minutes (30 minutes)

- ☐ Initiate important conversations. Write the name of a person you have been putting off a conversation with, the topic, and why it is important that you have that conversation.

  Who: _____

  Topic: _____

  Why: _____

- ☐ Pray for the patience to alleviate anxiety of the present, for the faith to reduce fear of the future, and the understanding, acceptance, grace, and forgiveness to ease guilt from the past.

Body: Sleep, Eat, and Exercise

☐ Sleep the number of hours recommended by The National Sleep Foundation. Go to sleepfoundation.org. Generally, you should sleep between seven to nine hours. Experiment with this for yourself to see what works best for you.

☐ Eat five meals at the following times: 7:00 a.m., 10:00 a.m. (snack), 12:00 p.m., 2:30 p.m. (snack), and 6:00 p.m.

☐ Exercise at 6:00 a.m. for 30 minutes

☐ Drink eight glasses of water. The 8 x 8 rule is easy to remember. Eight 8-ounce glasses a day. Dehydration can affect your mood, concentration, and brain function.

☐ Don't eat after 7:15 p.m.

☐ Limit sugar intake.

☐ Plan your meals every day and keep a food journal.

Wealth Attraction: Save and Invest

☐ Seek ways to save money. Track spending.

☐ Write ideas in your journal every day for wealth creation and actions needed to turn those ideas into reality.

☐ Invest your time, energy, and money wisely.

Profession:

- ☐ Determine my most important actions that generate income.
- ☐ Schedule my most important actions every 15 minutes.
- ☐ Always act on the most important thing I need to be doing. **Do what must be done now.**

Your Significance List consists of events, experiences, memories, your true purpose here on Earth, and the ultimate legacy that you will leave behind.

It also consists of your relationships with the most important people in your life: spouse/significant other, kids, parents, siblings, friends, etc.

Our lives are made up of relationships. The relationships we have with ourselves and other people determine our experiences, memories, and the story line of our lives.

Answer the following questions:

What does living a significant life mean to you?

_____

_____

Who are the most important people in your life?

_____

_____

Why is it important that you live a significant life?

_____

_____

How will you ensure that you live a significant life?

_____

_____

What's the biggest consequence of not living a significant life?

_____

_____

Significance List Examples:

Relationships: Interacting with People

- ☐ Conversations with people I care about, such as spouse/significant other, kids, parents, siblings, friends: _____

    _____

    _____

- ☐ Spend quality time with: _____

    _____

    _____

Parent:

- ☐ Teach my children something that will improve the quality of their life.
- ☐ Talk with them about their day.
- ☐ Pray with them.
- ☐ Challenge my children.

Purpose:

- ☐ My purpose today is to listen to someone that needs my attention and love.

- ☐ My purpose today is to create residual joy for another human being.

- ☐ My purpose today is to inspire someone to act on something that improves their quality of life.

- ☐ My purpose today is to transform a potentially painful situation into one that creates a positive outcome.

Spirituality:

- ☐ Pray for guidance so I always know the path to take. Pray for humility so that I may have respect. Pray for people to accept me for who I truly am. Pray for a clear perspective so that I can acquire wisdom to make smarter decisions every day. Pray for gratefulness so I will not become vain or bitter.

- ☐ Serve.

- ☐ Love.

Now that you have an idea of some things you can do to experience success and live a significant life, here are some templates for you to use daily to help you remember to plan the most important activities every morning.

You can use these as a panoramic view to plan your days. There are so many things we must do daily, so these templates will help you have everything in one place. Nothing falls between the cracks.

Success List

Health		Wealth	
Mind	**Body**	**Wealth**	**Profession**
Meditate for 10 minutes.	Exercise at 6:00 a.m.	Save money.	Prioritize activities.
Sleep 7–8 hours.	Eat five meals at 7:00, 10:30, 12:00, 2:30, and 6:00.	Use time wisely.	Schedule everything.
Ask yourself your focus questions.	Drink eight glasses of water. Keep a food journal.	Learn about money.	Act. Track time with scorecard.

Significance List

Relationships		Purpose	
People	**Love**	**Meaning**	**Experiences**
Spouse/ significant other	Show unconditional love. Give Communicate.	To Serve. To Make a difference.	Record the best memory of the day in your journal.
Children	Teach and lead.	To Share.	Enjoy the day.
Parents family members friends	Communicate.	To Love and connect.	Live in the moment.

Success List

Health		*Wealth*	
Mind	Body	Wealth	Profession

Significance List

Relationships		Purpose	
People	Love	Meaning	Experiences

PART 2: SUSTAINABILITY AND CONSISTENCY

"Trust is built with consistency."

—Lincoln Chafee

CHAPTER 6

Different Seasons, Different Reasons: Realize the Season of Life You're In

"ALL THE WORLD'S A STAGE, AND ALL THE MEN AND WOMEN MERELY PLAYERS: THEY HAVE THEIR EXITS AND THEIR ENTRANCES; AND ONE MAN IN HIS TIME PLAYS MANY PARTS, HIS ACTS BEING SEVEN AGES."

—WILLIAM SHAKESPEARE

What is preventing you from accomplishing all you want in business and life right now?

That question was asked to me and several of my colleagues several years ago at a semiannual planning session by our managing partner. Most of the twelve people in the room had different leadership positions within the company. As I sat watching and listening to the answers of each of my colleagues, I tried to think of how I was going to answer the question. I had just come out of a year where I had won Partner of the Year. My team of advisors had finished third in the entire country, and I had won the coveted View from the Top Award. Despite this, I was not performing at the level that I was capable of performing. As I sat there watching and listening to each of their responses, I heard a lot of different reasons or excuses. Mostly I heard why all these people thought they **weren't getting the results they wanted**. They said things like, "I don't have enough time." "I don't have the right systems." "Other people are not doing their part." "I don't have enough people to get it done." "I didn't manage my time properly." "We need a better process, better products, or better training."

As each person gave their response, the managing partner would say things like, "You are better than that!" That is what a good coach is supposed to say when a player on his team gives an excuse. He is supposed to hold them to a higher expectation.

I kept thinking to myself, *What will be my excuse as to why I am not performing at my best?* When it was my turn to answer the question, all the good excuses were used up. So I decided to tell the managing partner the truth. I said to Pat, "You know all those things have affected me at some point during my career, too. However, I must be honest with you. That's not what's holding me back right now. You know how competitive I am and how I hate not being number one. What's holding me back right now is the season of life that I am entering with my two boys, Jake and Reed, who are ten and eight.

"For me to win partner of the year again this year, I know that I am going to have to do more than I did last year. I'm not sure I'm willing to miss some really important moments that are going to be coming up with my boys in their sports and life."

It was tearing me apart inside because I was always somebody who earned great results. I now had to choose between being the best at work or spending time with my family.

The room was silent as I tried to hold back tears. The managing partner finally said, "He gets it. That's what life is about. It's about making experiences and memories, not just making money."

The current season of our life so often determines the reason we do things. Each season of your life shapes who you are and influences the next season of your life. To know how to outperform ourselves in business, school, sports, or anything else we do, we must first recognize what season of life we are in. We must become aware of what motivates us during different stages and ages of our personal and professional lives.

The season of life we are in affects our performance because of who we are at that stage of our life. For years I studied balance in life. As I grew older, I finally realized that true balance, in the sense that we spend equal time in each important area of our lives, is not likely going to happen. At different stages of our life, certain things will be more important than others. We will play many different roles in our lives as we progress from one season to the next. Our personal lives consist of seven seasons. Let's take a brief look at how different factors motivate us in each season.

SAILING THE SEVEN SEASONS OF OUR PERSONAL LIVES

Season 1: Building Blocks (Age 0–13)

Children learn at this age by watching what other people do. They are mostly influenced by their parents, teachers, coaches, friends, and family members. These years are the most formidable years. Children are like clay being molded and shaped into whatever the potter wants to mold them into. This is your best chance as a parent to impact the future of your child. Children at this age are usually seeking approval, acceptance, and love from their family and friends. Children learn trust or mistrust at this stage. It is one of the most important building blocks for a happy life. **They learn to trust what they see, not what they hear.**

Abraham Lincoln said, **"If you trust, you will be disappointed occasionally. If you mistrust, you will be miserable all the time."**

Season 2: The Identity Crisis (Age 13–22)

As teenagers and young adults, our parents, teachers, coaches, friends, and family members start to label us with things like smart, athletic, fast, slow, weird, shy, fat, skinny, popular, nerdy, and funny, just to name a few. If they say it enough, we start to believe it. This is the stage of life that we start to build a bank of beliefs about who we are. **We must be careful of what we believe about what other people say about us, or we may believe we are someone we are not.**

Hormones, seeking respect, selfishness, fame, fun, freedom, acceptance from peer groups, independence, social media such as Facebook, Twitter, Pinterest, and even video games are all strong driving forces that influence our behavior and routine in this season of our lives.

Season 3: The Relationship Season (Age 23–29)

Just as we get labeled when we are teenagers, we also get labeled when we are entering this season of life as we still struggle to find our identity. But this is usually **the season where our identity is shaped the most** because a lot of change occurs during this season. New careers are started, we move out on our own, possibly become a parent, possibly get married or end up in a serious relationship. The average age at which a person gets married in the US is 26.8 years for men, and 25.1 years for women. These are all major life events that shape who you become. We start to grow up because society expects us to by this point. Society now has a strong influence on who we become. Our parents still try to influence us, but we rebel as we seek independence and freedom. We seek to make our own mark on the world, express our individuality, and discover ourselves through experimentation and adventure.

The course of our lives, our careers, our identity, fitting in, and being recognized are all strong driving forces that influence our behavior and performance in this season of our lives.

Season 4: The Parenting Business and Business (Age 30–49)

Whether it is business or parenting, we start to want to build something that will outlive our lives. We want to accomplish great things. We are ready to take life to the next level. This is also when peak spending occurs, which is around age 46 or 47.

For a lot of parents today, their lives revolve around their children's lives. They seek to divide and conquer all they must do: sports, school functions, homework, birthday parties, church, fundraisers, dishes, laundry, cut the grass, clean the garage, pick up the dry cleaning, go to the bank, pay the bills, take out the trash, fix all the stuff that breaks at the worst possible time, find some time to play with the kids, walk the dog, watch your favorite TV show, go on a date night with your spouse, and talk to your mom on the phone. All this while trying to get ahead in your career. Sounds fun, doesn't it? If, on the other hand, you don't have children then you are probably focused on strengthening the other relationships you have in your life.

You may have a parent in this season of life that starts to experience health problems. This can affect your ability to outperform yourself because you must help, which is emotionally draining. During this season, **we are looking to find someone who can be a true friend that we can trust.**

Parenting, friendships, competition, building net worth, keeping up with the Joneses, accumulating things we have always wanted, and recognition for our efforts at work are strong driving forces during this season.

Season 5: The Freedom Season (Age 50–65)

Assuming you have survived the season before this one, you are now focused on learning how to enjoy the next season of your life without your children at home. If you don't have children, you are in the peak earning years of your career and should have earned some respect at work. You should have the financial stability and flexibility in your life to do more of the things you enjoy.

This is a particularly fun stage of life because you start to experience some freedom. Most people have saved some money and accumulated some of the things they want and are living in the home they want. The responsibilities have decreased unless you have a parent with health issues. The struggles we face here are the reality that our health doesn't generally get better as we get older. If you are like a lot of married people, you are learning to spend time with your spouse again after so many years of focusing on the kids. This can also be a time where you are finding your new identity. For so long you have been responsible for another human being and now you have some freedom from that responsibility.

Freedom, finances, health, and relationships are all strong driving forces during this season.

Season 6: Enjoying Life (Age 65–80)

This is the time we spend a lot of our lives talking about. We say, "When I retire, I am going to go fish, hunt, golf, spend time with the grandkids, or travel the world." You have arrived. And you start reflecting on your life personally, professionally, and spiritually. Some people think about what they could have done better and what they have accomplished. Some are looking to pass on their life experiences to the next generations. If all goes well, you have saved enough money to ride off into the sunset and live a life of success and significance, so you can leave a legacy to the next generation.

Driving forces that can affect quality of life are health, finance worries, relationships, regret, bitterness, sense of fulfillment, and feelings of wisdom.

Season 7: The Sage Age (Age 80+)

It's interesting how we start out life dependent on other people and we quite often end life dependent on other people. A select group of individuals will not have to be dependent on others if they have done what it takes to be healthy enough. Although some will be dependent on others during this last stage of their life, they still have a real opportunity to impact the world. They have seen so much happen over their lives and can pass on wisdom, experience, and history. Just think of how many events someone that is 100 years old has seen! People in this stage are very important because they hold the keys to the historical vaults in their minds. Many years of reflection and experience have formulated the treasured wisdom that this group possesses. If you are looking for a mentor, a true sage is a great place to start.

Driving factors in this stage of life are comfort, friendship, companionship, making sure you are at peace with God, wanting to leave a legacy, and family.

The important thing to remember when it comes to our personal and professional lives is that there are going to be times where we are limited by the season of life we are in. Anticipate, prepare, and plan for unexpected life events such as:

- Family members such as children, siblings, or parents getting sick
- Job loss
- Divorce
- Death of a loved one
- Disability
- Market downturn

Also recognize times when your life is going to limit your performance such as:

- Job Change
- New Baby
- Marriage

Enjoy life when events with children, family, and friends arise. Then work hard to achieve the lifestyle you desire.

Your level of success in life will be determined by the way you handle adversity when it strikes.

CHAPTER KEY NOTES

1. The current season of our life so often determines the reason we do things. Each season of your life shapes who you are and influences the next season of your life.

2. Children trust what they see, not what they hear.

3. We must be careful of what we believe about what other people say about us, or we may believe we are someone we are not.

4. The important thing to remember when it comes to our personal and professional lives is that there are going to be times where we are limited by the season of life we are in.

"Be who you are not who the world wants you to be."

—William Shakespeare

CHAPTER 7

The Single Most Important Discovery in Business:
Crusher, Rusher, Usher

"GET THE RIGHT PEOPLE ON THE BUS, THE WRONG PEOPLE OFF THE BUS,
AND THE RIGHT PEOPLE IN THE RIGHT SEATS."

—JIM COLLINS

In 1991, I was playing hockey in Moose Jaw Saskatchewan for Mike Babcock, the now two-time Olympic gold medal Canadian hockey coach and head coach of the Toronto Maple Leafs of the National Hockey League. As of November 2016, he is the only coach to gain entry to the Triple Gold Club by leading his team to the IIHF World Hockey Championship in 2004, the Detroit Red Wings to the Stanley Cup in 2008, as well as guiding Team Canada to gold at the 2010 Winter Olympics in Vancouver. He is the only coach to win five national or international titles, leading Canada to gold at the IIHF World Junior Championship in 1997 and the University of Lethbridge to a CIS National Championship in 1994. Babcock also led Team Canada at the 2014 Winter Olympics, successfully defending their gold medal. He also led Team Canada to another championship in 2016 at the IIHF World Hockey Championship.

One day after practice, Mike called me into his office to talk. He asked me if I knew what my role on the team was. At 18 years old I wasn't sure of anything, so out of fear of saying the wrong thing, I said, "I'm not sure."

He then told me a story about a coach he played for who told him that if you are a crusher and you try to be a rusher, you will become an usher. This meant that if I tried to rush the puck up the ice and be a rusher to score a goal instead of being a crusher, who is a physical hard-nosed player, then I would be sitting in the stands and playing the role of an usher. In other words, start playing your role or you'll be sitting in the stands.

Do you know what your role is in your organization? This is one of the most important factors in outperforming yourself in business.

In the book *Good to Great,* Jim Collins says, "Get the right people on the bus, the wrong people off the bus, and the right people in the right seats."

This is essentially the single-most important discovery in business or sports. The right PEOPLE in the right ROLES drive results.

I believe we have all known this for years. However, when a great new technology comes along, a new strategy for doing business, or a revolutionary new product, we lose sight of the real reason why organizations, sports teams, or companies are successful. **They have the right people doing what they are gifted at.**

This point can be demonstrated simply by eliminating each factor that drives business forward. You quickly find out that without the right people, your business will struggle more than if you get rid of your client relationship management system, technology, machines, business plans, buildings, or even your products or services. **There are very few companies that can continue to exist and flourish without the right people.**

This is easily highlighted and illustrated in sports. If you have all the best equipment, the nicest arena, the best jerseys, and largest salary cap, none of that matters if you don't have great players. You must also have players that can fill all the roles for your team to win a championship. A great example of this was the 2015 NBA Championship where the Golden State Warriors defeated the Cleveland Cavaliers. Or should I say Lebron James?

Lebron James is one of the greatest players to ever play the game of basketball. However, it was not enough to beat the Golden State Warriors, who had all the right people in all the right roles.

So how do you become the right person in the right role within your organization, your company, or on your team?

How do you decide who you want to be when you're not sure who you are? I believe we have an identity crisis going on in the world today. So many people don't know who they truly want to be. They have lost sight of the future because of the busyness of life, and their job is just something that pays the bills; it's not their dream job.

It's hard when we are being influenced by so many things like media, technology, friends, family, culture, Facebook, Twitter, LinkedIn, teachers, leaders, coaches, children, colleagues, and businesses, just to name a few. How can you know where you are going in life if you don't know who you are?

High performance in business all starts with your level of passion. Find out what you are passionate about and what you are naturally gifted at. I am sure you have heard the statement before: *Do what you love, and love what you do.* When you love what you do, you will never work another day in your life.

When you find your obsession, make it your profession.

OB·SES·SION

A PERSISTENT IDEA OR IMPULSE THAT CONTINUALLY FORCES ITS WAY INTO CONSCIOUSNESS, OFTEN ASSOCIATED WITH ANXIETY AND MENTAL ILLNESS.

Okay, we don't want the anxiety and mental illness part. What if we had a positive natural impulse that was forcing its way into our mind? You wouldn't have to force yourself to do what it takes to be successful because you would naturally want to do it. It's like a professional athlete playing a sport they love.

Your instinct is to do what you love, so why not figure out a way to do it all day? I am asking you: *what could you do within your current role or profession that would be the best fit for your talents and desires?* Your talents tend to follow your desires because you tend to be good at what you consistently think about or practice. Sometimes the best way to find out our obsession or passion is to ask other people. I was fortunate to have a great coach that helped me see what my gifts and talents were.

Knowing who you truly are is the most important discovery of your lifetime. When you find out who that person is, I truly believe they are the only person that can turn your life around.

When I changed firms a few years back, I remember telling someone the reason I changed firms was because I was the best where I was, but I wasn't being the best that I could be. I wanted to be the best that I could be, not just the best where I was.

Decide today to commit to the role you were meant to play in your life and business and become the best that you can be in each of those roles.

CHAPTER KEY NOTES

1. The right PEOPLE in the right ROLES drive results.

2. There are very few companies that can continue to exist and flourish without the right people.

3. When you find your obsession, make it your profession.

4. Knowing who you truly are is the most important discovery of your lifetime. When you find out who that person is, I truly believe they are the only person that can turn your life around.

"Find the gift of passion."

—Mike Babcock, Coach of Team Canada

CHAPTER 8

Unlearning Learned Behaviors: Limiting Habits and Limiting Beliefs

"THE PAST IS HISTORY, THE FUTURE IS A MYSTERY, AND TODAY IS A GIFT, THAT'S WHY THEY CALL IT THE PRESENT."

— ANONYMOUS

"What I'd like for you to do is change everything about yourself and get back to me."

There are three ways to predict future performance and behaviors.

1. Past behavior: What beliefs, habits, and environments caused you to behave the way you did?

2. Current behavior: What beliefs, habits, and environments are currently influencing your decisions?

3. Future behavior: How is your attitude? What are you focusing on?

It's imperative that you know what drove your behaviors that limited your results in the past. You can prevent the past from happening repeatedly like in the movie *Groundhog Day*.

You arrived here **by choosing to be** the person you have been in the past, and you will get wherever you are going by choosing to be whomever you **choose to be** in the future. **You make many decisions in life. Choose wisely. It determines your results, which determines your destiny.**

According to the internet, humans make approximately 35,000 conscious decisions a day. Of course, this varies vastly depending on the person and their circumstances. For example, a child only makes about 3,000 conscious decisions a day.

There are two ways we make decisions: conscious and unconscious.

The best way to make better decisions on a conscious level is to be aware of the consequences of our decision. By being aware of the outcome of the decision, we can rationalize whether to act.

The second way we make decisions is on an unconscious level. This one is a little bit trickier because we are not always aware of the decision we are making. These decisions can be influenced by our innate habits and beliefs.

Let me ask you a question. Have you ever been burned?

When someone gets burned, they quickly learn that whatever

burned them is hot and it hurts. So the next time they get close to a burner, stove, or fire, their brain tells them *"Danger ahead! Don't go there!"* This is a belief that is engrained into their mind. But sometimes beliefs like this can be wrong because a stove or burner is not always hot.

The same thing happens with sales people. When they make calls and have a negative experience, their brain links up pain to making calls. This is called a limiting belief. We know that not all sales calls bring pain. Some can bring great joy and happiness. We must realize that the meaning we give to an experience is not always going to be the same every time. If you can get in the habit of making good conscious decisions based on accurate and relevant information, you can master your life.

Becoming aware of our limiting habits and beliefs and how they affect our decision-making process helps us get unstuck from our own patterns of behavior so we can get ahead in life.

So often people ask the question, "How do I become successful?" They really should be asking themselves, "What is preventing me from becoming successful?" Most people know what it takes to get great results. They just aren't doing it. Why?

The answer is limiting habits and limiting beliefs, which cause you to make decisions that don't create the results you want.

Limiting beliefs cause us to doubt. Limiting habits cause us to not act, which affects our results.

In this chapter, we will identify the internal or external, subconscious or conscious, voluntary or involuntary, innate or learned **beliefs, behaviors, emotions, habits, environments, people, actions, and attitudes** that are affecting your results.

I have listed some definitions that affect our decision-making process daily.

Action: A conscious activity which has a subjective goal for the environment or person involved.

Attitude: The way we think or feel towards others or situations.

Behavior: Innate human actions we take based on stimulus, thoughts, and belief systems.

Belief: An opinion of what we believe to be true based on our experiences.

Emotion: A feeling invoked by an experience.

Environment: External surroundings, forces, things, cultures, and conditions that influence our world.

Habit: A higher cognitive process acquired through consistent conditioning until it becomes involuntary or a regular routine.

Intention: Purpose toward a desired outcome.

People: Members of humanity who are influencing and persuading you.

Thoughts: An idea or opinion produced by thinking or occurring suddenly in the mind.

Below are **samples** to help you brainstorm your list that you want to change:

Actions: blaming, rolling eyes, frowning, guilt tripping, being impulsive, insulting, gossiping, fighting, arguing, hating, manipulating, judging, procrastinating, lying, cheating, stealing

Attitudes: rebellious, negative, rude, guarded, ungrateful, arrogant, indifferent, envious, pessimistic, jealous, disrespectful, irresponsible, entitled, unwilling, impatient, selfish, stubborn

Behaviors: dramatic, naysaying, contempt, criticism, stonewalling, defensiveness, manipulation, bad manners, wasting time, wasting energy, wasting money, morality, intolerance, unforgiving, selfishness, poor listening

Beliefs: past mistakes, not good enough, too young, too old, not enough time, inexperienced, it's impossible, doubt, fear, unwanted, not smart enough, no money, my fault, circumstances, unattractive, flawed, rejected

Emotions: anxiety, stress, fear, depression, anger, resentment, frustration, regret, guilt, uncertainty, aggravation, embarrassment

Environments: work, home, community

Habits: smoking, drinking, drug use, not getting enough sleep, not exercising, poor diet, not scheduling, lying, cheating, swearing, picking your nose (just kidding, I was making sure you're still reading), biting finger nails, emotional shopping

Intentions: causing harm, suffering, or negative emotions for another

People: toxic relationships with parents, friends, family, coworkers, associations, neighbors, teams, organizations, and/or religious groups

Thoughts: fear, despair, terror, useless, confused, humiliation, doubt, powerless, disappointed, guilt, anxious, lonely, nervous, resentful, regret, panic, pathetic, bitter, sadness, depressed

If you can't think of anything you need to change about yourself, ask your close friends, family, spouse, or significant other, "What three things would you change about me?" Ask them to be honest. Also ask them, "What do you love about me?" If they're able to end it on a good note, they won't feel as bad telling you things they would change.

This is going to be your new **Not To Do List**. So often we create to do lists when we really should be thinking about things we should eliminate. This way we can live a simplified life. By trying to become more, you become less.

It has been proven that when you have less choices to choose from, you make better decisions. Too many choices can be overwhelming. Let's begin this exercise now to make your life easier. You can reference the list on the previous pages if you need to brainstorm things you want to change.

Three step processes to change anything now:

1. Awareness
2. Caring
3. Support

Awareness is the first key to change. If you are not aware of what you need to change, then you will probably never change it.

Once you are aware, you must ask yourself, "Do I care if I change this?" If there is not enough pain linked to changing the behavior, you will probably not change.

Lastly, change without support rarely works. You need to surround yourself with people that want to see you succeed and will motivate you when you need it. They will hold you accountable to what needs to be done for you to win.

Identify any of the following that are limiting your life in any way:

☐ **Action I am eliminating:**

_____

☐ **Attitude I am eliminating:**

_____

☐ **Behavior I am eliminating:**

_____

☐ **Belief I am eliminating:**

_____

☐ **Emotion I am eliminating:**

_____

☐ **Environment I am eliminating:**

_____

☐ **Habit I am eliminating:**

_____

☐ **Intention I am eliminating:**

_____

☐ **Toxic relationship I am eliminating:**

_____

☐ **Thought I am eliminating:**

_____

Revisit this chapter when you have conquered or mastered any of the above and check off the ones you have completed.

Being aware of pain associated with making poor decisions greatly impacts behavior.

"Your net worth to the world is usually determined by what remains after your bad habits are subtracted from your good ones"

—BENJAMIN FRANKLIN

CHAPTER 9

Installing New Habits, Beliefs, and Behaviors

"WITHOUT SUPPORT, CHANGE IN BEHAVIOR BECOMES EXTINCT."

—SUSAN SCOTT

Now that you **recognize what has stopped you from getting the results you've wanted in the past,** it's time to recognize **what will determine your results in the future.**

Your results in life are largely determined by being moved enough to act and be self-controlled enough to live your life in a way that consistently creates the results you want.

So often people don't take time to find their true passion, therefore they end up living an unfulfilled life.

With the right amount of passion and discipline, you can accomplish anything you want in life.

Passion and discipline have a greater impact on results than knowledge.

So what drives results?

You do!

You must have a vision that is powerful enough to ignite your passion to get you to change your focus, habits, beliefs, emotions, sense of urgency, commitment level, the people you surround yourself with, and environment.

Whenever you eliminate something from your life, like you just did in the previous chapter, it's a good idea to replace the void with something else. It's like when people quit smoking they need to have something to replace the oral fixation.

In the previous chapter, you created a **Not To Do List**. Now create your new list of actions, attitudes, behaviors, beliefs, emotions, environments, habits, intentions, people, and thoughts that create the quality of life and freedom you desire.

Below are **samples** to help you brainstorm your new list that will help you replace your old patterns:

Actions: empowering and encouraging others, taking responsibility, using affirmative language, showing patience, demonstrating courage, being kind, loving, collaborating, guiding, helping, smiling, affectionate

Attitudes: joyful, positive, caring, encouraging, grateful, honest, respectful, responsible, selfless, optimistic, open-minded, trusting, devoted, sympathetic

Behaviors: funny, enthusiastic, loyal, being attentive

Beliefs: there is always a way if I am committed, hard work and patience will pay off, my past does not dictate my future, with the right amount of passion and discipline I can accomplish anything I want

Emotions: peace, serenity, faith, hope, joy, happiness, gratitude, bliss, acceptance, satisfaction, certainty, confidence, accomplishment, security, abundance

Environments: work, home, community, relationships, parenting, family

Habits: the right amount of sleep, exercise, diet, scheduling, practicing, learning, eating right, meditating, praying

Intentions: loving, turning negative energy into positive energy

People: parents, friends, family, coworkers, associations, neighbors, teams, organizations, religious groups

Thoughts: faith, hope, happiness, peace, joy, empowered, serenity, bliss, grateful

Now identify the new replacements for your old habits or behaviors:

☐ **New Action:**

_____

☐ **New Attitude:**

_____

☐ **New Behavior:**

_____

☐ **New Belief:**

_____

☐ **New Emotion:**

_____

☐ **New Environments:**

_____

☐ **New Habit:**

_____

☐ **New Intention:**

_____

☐ **New Mentor For An Area In My Life I Need Help With:**

_____

☐ **New Thought:**

_____

Now print out the new list and put it in a place where you will see it all day if possible. **When you control your focus, you control the momentum of your life.**

CHAPTER KEY NOTES

1. Your results in life are largely determined by being moved enough to act and be self-controlled enough to live your life in a way that consistently creates the results you want.

2. With the right amount of passion and discipline, you can accomplish anything you want in life.

3. Passion and discipline have a greater impact on results than knowledge.

4. Whenever you eliminate something from your life, like you just did in the previous chapter, it's a good idea to replace the void with something else.

5. When you control your focus, you control the momentum of your life.

"All human actions have one or more of these seven causes: chance, nature, compulsions, habit, reason, passion and desire."

—Aristotle

CHAPTER 10

Building Your Dream Team

"COORDINATION OF KNOWLEDGE AND EFFORT, IN A SPIRIT OF HARMONY, BETWEEN TWO OR MORE PEOPLE, FOR THE ATTAINMENT OF A DEFINITE PURPOSE."

—NAPOLEON HILL

Designing and constructing your own Dream Team is **the fastest way** to acquire the accumulated knowledge, research, experience, strategies, ideas, and wisdom that is crucial to your success in business and in life.

I want you to imagine for a minute that you are sitting in a room with Jesus, Albert Einstein, Mahatma Gandhi, Stephen Covey, Tony Robbins, John Wooden, Bill Gates, Mother Theresa, Aristotle, William Shakespeare, Buddha, Warren Buffet, Oprah Winfrey, Confucius, Plato, and the Dalai Lama. Now think to yourself, *How long would it take for me learn everything that these people know?* Is it safe to say that you could learn more in one hour with a group like this than you may be able to learn in your entire lifetime on your own?

If that's true, then why are you not surrounding yourself with successful people on a regular basis?

It could simply be that you are not aware of this powerful strategy for acquiring the knowledge, experience, wisdom, and intellect that you need to be successful. It could be that you think you are too busy to start a group like this.

Think about this: the consequences of not having the kind of conversations you could have in a group like this *can be costly.* You could be missing out on information that could change your life and your business in a big way. So what is the best way to start a group like this? I am going to share with you my own experience and proven method for starting your very own Dream Team.

The first question you must ask yourself is: *What is the purpose of my group?*

Your vision statement might sound something like this:

Our Dream Team exists to be a collective group of independent thinkers working interdependently to discover fresh, new innovative ways to solve our most difficult business problems, conquer challenges, and capitalize on opportunities.

We examine the reality to uncover hidden truths, opinions, beliefs, and attitudes.

We convert thoughts into actions and ideas into reality.

We design and act upon plans that will improve our results immediately.

We learn from other people's experiences so we don't have to waste time, energy, and money making the same mistakes.

We share accumulated knowledge, research, experience, strategies, and wisdom.

We delve into creative thinking to build better processes that get us better results.

We dream of new ideas that can be executed to generate multiple streams of income.

We imagine new possibilities that can impact and enhance our lives.

We work in concert to get projects done faster.

We hold each other accountable to our own vision.

We lead each other to a better future.

We align strategy with action plans now.

Once you have a definite super purpose for your Dream Team then you must select your team. This is done using the same means you would use to build a sports franchise. Think of who the most important players would be on your team. If you were building a baseball team you would need a pitcher, catcher, first baseman, and so on. When selecting this team, you will want to consider what type of people you will need and want in the group. What you want is a group of people that all think in different ways with multiple competing views from different professions, age groups, genders, cultural backgrounds, and geographies. Think about this for a second: what generally happens at one of your industry meetings? The first couple times you go, you probably get some good ideas. Then you start to hear the same answer to the same problem repeatedly because most people in that industry think the same way. This is not a bad thing. It's just that **you are not going to grow if you keep thinking the same way.**

The six main categories to consider when building your Dream Team are:

1. Gender
2. Demographic
3. Geographic
4. Cultural
5. Professions
6. Attitude, Beliefs, and Opinions

An ideal Dream Team might look something like this:

GENDER

No doubt that men and women think differently. The goal here is to have as many people as possible that have competing realities. If you are married or in a relationship you know how this one works.

4 men

4 women

DEMOGRAPHICS: AGE GROUPS

1–2 people in their 20s. This is the next generation that can give you a fresh, new innovative insight into the future.

1–2 people in their 30s. Generally, these people can be newlyweds or new parents. They are in the beginning stages of starting to grow their wealth. People change a lot in their early 30s. Change teaches us life lessons that can be valuable to your group.

1–2 people in their 40s. These people are generally highly motivated and ready to accelerate their careers. This is an age group where peak spending usually occurs at around age 46. Their skill set is also peaking, which usually allows them to be in influential positions within their organizations.

1–2 people in their 50s. People in their 50s have had enough time to figure out what works and what doesn't. They can base their judgment calls on experience and wisdom, not on theory.

1–2 people in their 60s, 70s, 80s, 90s, or even 100+. This is the wisdom group. Having someone from this age group is essential because they generally have the most accumulated knowledge, experience, and wisdom of any of the groups. They tend to be more patient and make decisions based on logic.

GEOGRAPHIC

Having people from different areas of your region, country, or the world can enhance the quality of your group because different geographies have their own unique challenges, opportunities, and perspectives.

CULTURAL

Diversity is the goal here. A multi-cultural group offers the opportunity to peek inside the minds of people who have a mixture of beliefs, attitudes, experiences, religious viewpoints, and a distinctive way of life.

PROFESSIONS

Selecting the right professions is significant for several reasons. The right balance of professions creates synergy that will give your group common interests and goals. Working towards a common goal unites the group and helps keep the group together long term.

When constructing your Dream Team, you might consider choosing some people from the following industries:

- Technology
- Health Care
- Legal
- Financial: actuaries, risk management, wealth advisors, insurers, bankers
- Education: professors, teachers, headmasters, principals
- Manufacturing
- Religious Leaders
- Professional Speakers
- Business Owners
- Government: politicians

- Coaches
- Athletes
- Writers
- Entertainment Industry
- Advertising

There are many professions I have not listed that could be included this list. It is simply provided to help you brainstorm your initial core group.

ATTITUDE, BELIEFS, AND OPINIONS

This category will influence your group more than anything else, so it is the most important category to consider. It is imperative that you choose wisely here. When I was designing my group, I ran into an issue that many of you may run into.

The issue is this: how do you **select and deselect** members of the group? This can be difficult because you may have people that you really want to have in the group, but they are not a good fit at that time. You may want to go against your instincts and add them to the group because of their reputation, status, or friendship. **Never disobey your instincts.**

When building our group, this is what we did: at least two founding members went out and interviewed each potential candidate and communicated to them the intent of the group, and, more importantly, the expectations.

Then we asked ourselves after meeting with them if they would be the best person we could add to the group. Our rule is simple for adding people. It goes like this: You know how when you ask someone a question and they hesitate? You know something isn't right. If there is any hesitation of any kind, we do not add them to the group. If we say to ourselves, "This person would be awesome, we must have them," then we ask them to join us.

Basically, **we obey our instincts.**

Clearly defining our expectations is crucial to the long-term sustainability of the group.

Here are some of the expectations we have in our group:

Attendance: If you are going to be absent from a meeting, you must notify someone in the group. If you miss three consecutive meetings without notifying someone, you are automatically giving up your spot in the group. In other words, three strikes and you're out.

Contribution: If you are not getting anything out of the group, it doesn't make sense for you to be in the group. To get the best results in a group like this, everyone that is there needs to contribute in some way.

Respect: It is expected that you will always seek to earn the respect of your peers through expressions of gratitude for their contribution, honoring their time by not wasting it, and not judging their perspectives.

Privacy: Boundaries surrounding intellectual property, content, and sensitive and private information should be clearly defined before you begin. Some groups sign a non-disclosure agreement if they feel like it is necessary.

Trust: It is very important you have confidence that you can rely on each member of your group. Having competent, honest, capable, talented, and wise people in your group is the key to having trust in your group. The right people are going to drive results. Choose wisely.

Mindset: The group should share a common vision and state of mind.

The unique thing that happens in a mastermind group is when an idea materializes not because of something you said or something someone else said, it just appears in the air like a thought bubble in a cartoon.

The mastermind does not exist without the collective thoughts of the group.

I was at a mastermind meeting with Kevin Eastman, the assistant basketball coach for the Los Angeles Clippers in Los Angeles, and he made the comment, "I only know what I know, and if I only know what I know, then I need to know what you know."

I realized at that moment that as successful as Kevin has been in winning an NBA Championship, you can always learn from other people and their experiences regardless of how successful you are or become.

That is what the Dream Team concept is all about. Surround yourself with people that can help you grow to a level that you could not grow to on your own.

Are you ready to take your life to the next level? Are you at that point in your life where you want to become the person you know you are meant to be? Only you can answer that question. If you are ready, then you must decide to accept the things you cannot change and focus on the things you can. Move forward towards your ideal life.

Remember to enjoy the journey and leave a path of residual joy everywhere you go.

Life Mastery Assessment

The purpose of this quick assessment is to help you identify any of the **seven key areas of Life Mastery** that may be limiting your results and preventing you from getting what you want in any area of your life.

The way it works is you pick one area of your life, which could be your profession, relationship with your kids/spouse/significant other, health, finances, etc. Then do a self-assessment to determine which area of Life Mastery is preventing you from mastering that area of your life.

Take the assessment.

Choose one area of life you want to improve now:

- ☐ Profession
- ☐ Finances
- ☐ Health
- ☐ Parenting
- ☐ Relationship
- ☐ Emotions

The seven key areas of Life Mastery

How would you rate yourself on a scale of 1 to 5 in each of the following areas in the area of life you want to improve?

KNOWLEDGE

Knowledge: *Facts and information acquired through experience, experimentation, or education; the theoretical or practical understanding of a subject.*

How would you rate your overall thirst for knowledge of the subject you are wanting to improve?

Circle one:

1   2   3   4   5

Tip: The **3 E's (Experience, Experimentation, or Education)** can help you acquire the knowledge you need to be successful. Always be learning.

Write down one thing you can do to improve this area of your life and when you will do it.

One Thing: _____

_____

Date & Time: _____

SKILL

Skill: *The ability to do something well; expertise acquired through practice, conditioning, and preparation.*

How would you rate your overall skill in the area you are wanting to improve?

Circle one:

1 2 3 4 5

Tip: To improve your skills in anything, **daily practice and preparation** will help you master your skills in any area of your life.

Write down one thing you can do to improve this area of your life and when you will do it.

One Thing: _____

_____

Date & Time: _____

TIME

Time: *Time is a measurement of how long it takes to complete an event or task. It is a measurement of how much time we spend daily doing certain things.*

How would you rate your overall use of time in the area you are wanting to improve? In other words, how much time do you invest in self-improvement? Are you utilizing your time wisely in this area?

Circle one:

1   2   3   4   5

Tip: To improve your use of your time you must use **discipline and focus** to master this. Use the focus formulas in this book and other techniques outlined in the *I Am Conditioning* chapter.

Write down one thing you can do to improve this area of your life and when you will do it.

One Thing: _____

_____

Date & Time: _____

DESIRE

Desire: *Desire is how bad you want something. The internal and external motivation behind why we act.*

How would you rate your overall desire in the area you are wanting to improve? Are you highly motivated to get the best results you can in this area of your life?

Circle one:

1   2   3   4   5

Tip: Desire can be obtained by **clarifying and focusing** on what your purpose and passion are.

Write down one thing you can do to improve this area of your life and when you will do it.

One Thing: _____

_____

Date & Time: _____

HABITS

Habit: *A higher cognitive process acquired through consistent conditioning until it becomes involuntary or a regular routine.*

How would you rate your overall habits in the area you are wanting to improve?

Circle one:

1   2   3   4   5

Tip: Habits are changed one day and one decision at a time. **Consistent conditioning** creates an environment for involuntary habits to form and stick.

Write down one thing you can do to improve this area of your life and when you will do it.

One Thing: _____

_____

Date & Time: _____

BELIEFS

Beliefs: *A thought based on a bank of past experiences. Trust and sometimes accept that your thoughts are true. It is the meaning you give to experiences.*

How would you rate your beliefs in the area you are wanting to improve?

Circle one:

1   2   3   4   5

Tip: The fastest way to change your beliefs is to **change the meaning of an experience in your mind.** The second way to change your beliefs is to **change your experiences** related to those beliefs.

Write down one thing you can do to improve this area of your life and when you will do it.

One Thing: _____

_____

Date & Time: _____

SEASON OF LIFE

Season of Life: *Where you currently are on your journey through life.*

How would you rate yourself on how well you are adjusting to the season of life you are currently in?

Circle one:

1   2   3   4   5

Tip: This is one of the seven key areas that is mostly out of your control. However, there are two things you can do to improve this area of life especially if you are in a busy season of life. **Diligently schedule** as much as you can and only **focus on what you can control.** This can help lower your stress and provide more clarity and certainty in your life.

Write down one thing you can do to improve this area of your life and when you will do it.

One Thing: _____

_____

Date & Time: _____

Scorecard

Life Mastery Area	Score
Knowledge	
Skill	
Time	
Desire	
Habits	
Beliefs	
Season of Life	
Overall Score	

Now that you have finished the assessment, go back and look over your answers and pick the one that you know that if you **improved this area of Life Mastery right now** you will **immediately start to make progress towards improving this area of your life.** Now go to work on that one thing today.

Remember: progress to perfection is by moving in the right direction.

With the right amount of passion and discipline, you can accomplish anything.

Recommended Reading

CONVERSATIONS/LEADERSHIP

Fierce Conversations: Achieving Success at Work and in Life, One Conversation at a Time by Susan Scott

Fierce Leadership: A Bold Alternative to the Worst "Best" Practices of Business Today by Susan Scott

RELATIONSHIPS/LOVE

The Love Dare by Stephen Kendrick and Alex Kendrick

BUSINESS

The Speed of Trust: The One Thing That Changes Everything by Stephen Covey

VISION

Start with Why: How Great Leaders Inspire Everyone to Take Action by Simon Sinek

MONEY

MONEY Master the Game: 7 Simple Steps to Financial Freedom by Tony Robbins

HEALTH

Ageless Body, Timeless Mind: The Quantum Alternative to Growing Old by Deepak Chopra

SALES

How to Win Friends and Influence People by Dale Carnegie

NEGOTIATION

The 3rd Alternative: Solving Life's Most Difficult Problems by Stephen Covey

Acknowledgements

To all the people that believed in me when I didn't believe in myself so that I could believe in myself again. To all the people that gave me a chance when I was starting out.

FAMILY

Specifically, I am forever grateful to my mom for bringing me into this world when she was 16 years old, single, and broke. Thank you for teaching me to never give up no matter how bad things get.

Thank you to my dad for teaching me that with patience and hard work you can overcome anything.

Thank you to my grandmother who taught me to always be kind and compassionate to other people.

Thank you to Jake and Reed for being the inspiration behind why I work so hard to set a good example for you guys to live by.

THANK YOU TO ALL THE GREAT COACHES I PLAYED FOR.

Mike Babcock, thanks for the crusher, rusher, usher story.

Jack Capuano, thanks for being there for me when I lost my sight and for giving me a second chance to come back and play after my injury.

Brent Fudge, thanks for calling me up based on my work ethic and not on my talent, and thanks for putting me in the game in double overtime to win the game for that one shift.

Bryan Maxwell, thanks for teaching me the value of preparation, hard work, and how to be a champion.

Don Nachbaur, thanks for believing in me to be one of the captains of one of the greatest Seattle teams ever.

BUSINESS MENTORS

Steve Adkins, thank you for not giving up on me when I was about to give up on myself and for the many wise lessons you taught me about people and business.

Raeanne Lacatena, thank you for your guidance and friendship during one of the toughest times in my life.

Pat McCraw, thank you for showing me how to hold people accountable in a loving way.

Mandi Stanley for the conversation we had many years ago that ignited me to start doing coaching, consulting, and speaking.

Kurt Black for all the time we have spent together building Champion Advisor.

LIFE MENTOR

Dr. Chandra Persaud is one of the wisest people I've met and has educated me so much about life through our candid conversations. She has helped me appreciate that life is not about making money and always being successful. It is okay to fail and suffer. It's a part of life. It makes us who we are.

PEOPLE THAT HELPED MAKE THIS BOOK A REALITY

CJ, thank you for all your reviews of the book content. You are amazing and brilliant. I appreciate you so much for all the time you spent helping me.

Sheenah, my book editor and cover designer, for your wisdom, creativity, passion for books, and patience. You are awesome and made publishing this book easy. You're the best.

About the Author

Dave Jesiolowski leads a global training and coaching organization that specializes in working with entrepreneurs, financial services professionals, athletes, and influencers to help them become world-class champions. Dave has accumulated strategies over the last three decades from being a professional hockey player, a world-class champion in two Fortune 500 companies, an author, and a speaker. He trained in the Tony Robbins coaching certification program and he was coached by the legendary Mike Babcock, a Stanley Cup champion and two-time Olympic gold medal winner.

For more information visit:
DaveJesiolowski.com

Made in the USA
Columbia, SC
19 August 2023

21807632R00083